1100 1200 1300 1400 1500 1600 1700 1800 1900 2000

CANADA THROUGH TIME

Pioneer Life

Kathleen Corrigan

capstone

Read Me is published by Heinemann Raintree,
an imprint of Capstone Press,
1710 Roe Crest Drive, North Mankato, Minnesota 56003

© 2016 Heinemann-Raintree
an imprint of Capstone Global Library, LLC
Chicago, Illinois

To contact Capstone please visit www.mycapstone.com

Edited by James Benefield
Designed by Philippa Jenkins
Original illustrations © Capstone Global Library Ltd 2016
Picture research by Kelly Garvin
Production by Victoria Fitzgerald
Originated by Capstone Global Library Limited

ISBN 978 1 410 98118 9 (hardback)
ISBN 978 1 410 98123 3 (paperback)
ISBN 978 1 410 98128 8 (ebook)
ISBN 978-1-4109-8295-7 (saddle stitch)

Acknowledgments
Photo credits: Alamy: age footstock, 18, Chronicle, 21, canadabrian, 11, Cliff LeSergent, 7, Malcolm McMillan, 25, Marshall Ikonography, 15, 16, National Geographic Image Collection, 23; Capstone Press/Karon Dubke, 28, 29; Corbis: Leonard de Selva, 14, Scott T. Smith, 6; Granger, NYC, cover (bottom), 17; Library and Archives Canada: Canadian National Railways, C-016926, 10, Henry Joseph Woodside, PA-016543, 19, PA-044842, cover (top), PA-074670, 27; Library of Congress/Print & Photographs Division, 26; North Wind Picture Archives, 5, 9, 12, 13, 22, 24; Shutterstock: ehrlif, 8, Maria Dryfhout, 20.

Printed in the United States of America.
102016   010093RP

Some words are shown in bold, **like this**. You can find out what they mean by looking in the glossary.

Contents

The first pioneers

Pioneers were people who came to Canada from another country. They made their new homes in the **wilderness**. Pioneers began to settle and claim land around 400 years ago. They had to work very hard when they arrived.

Some pioneers settled in Upper and Lower Canada.

Lower Canada

Upper Canada

UNITED STATES OF AMERICA

The first pioneers mostly built log cabins or shacks to live in. They used logs from nearby forests. A cabin might have had only one room and a dirt floor. A fireplace was used to cook food and heat the cabin.

Later pioneers built homes with wood planks. These homes might have had three or four rooms and glass windows.

Sometimes pioneers ate, slept, and lived in just one room.

Some pioneer cabins were very small.

Clearing the land

Pioneers cleared their land so they could farm. They cut down trees and took tree stumps and rocks out of the ground.

Pioneers plowed the soil so they could then plant seeds and **harvest crops**. Sometimes they planted around big things because they didn't have the tools or time to dig out.

Pioneers sometimes used thin tree trunks to make fences.

Pioneer men and women had to work very hard to clear enough land to plant crops.

Growing food

Pioneers grew most of their own food. They planted fruit, vegetables, flowers, and herbs. In their plowed fields they planted **crops** like corn, rye, oats, wheat, and **flax**. They would either eat these crops or trade them with other pioneers or **First Nations** people.

Pioneer children helped their parents in the fields.

DID YOU KNOW?

Pioneers dried hay and straw for their animals. They also had to dry, pickle, smoke, or salt food. This helped to keep the food fresh during the winter when no crops could be grown.

Hunting food

Pioneers also went hunting for food. The men hunted animals such as deer and ducks or went fishing. The meat was cooked and then eaten or dried for winter. Women and children **foraged** for plants and berries. It took a lot of hard work to make a pioneer meal!

The pioneers used many parts of the animals they hunted or farmed. For example, they made clothing from animal skin or fur.

DID YOU KNOW?

Pioneers cooked their food over a fire. They used iron pots and kettles. Bread was baked in an oven that was built into the side of the fireplace.

People in different places

Many pioneers lived far away from a town. They might go there only once or twice a year. Some families lived closer, so they could go to the school, church, and stores. Children far from a school might learn at home. Some did not learn to read.

Some pioneers lived in huts by water.

The general store sold things the pioneers could not make or grow, such as needles and thread, tea, sugar, dishes, and candy.

Town life

Between 1750 and 1850, the pioneers began to build more towns. The towns were usually built near water. People could travel by boat between towns, and they could use the water to make their **mills** work. Many people worked in towns, for example, blacksmiths.

Blacksmiths made things from metal, such as tools and horseshoes.

DID YOU KNOW?

There were many machines in towns. Millers used machines to help do their work. Gristmills ground flour and sawmills made planks of wood.

Pioneer schools

Many pioneer schools had only one room. The children had to work silently except when the teacher spoke to them. Children got up early to do **chores** before they went to school. They might milk the cows, collect eggs, or help cook. Children had chores at school too, such as bringing in firewood or cleaning desks.

At school, one teacher taught all the grades.

This school at Bear Creek
was just one room.

Pioneer clothes

Many pioneers had few clothes. A boy might have two shirts and two pairs of pants. A girl might have two **aprons**, a dress, and a **bonnet**. It was hard work to wash clothes, so children wore the same clothes for many days.

Old clothes were saved and the cloth was used to make rugs and quilts.

Pioneers made their clothes. They used animal skins, wool, and linen. They also repaired their own clothing.

Family life

Pioneer children helped their families every day. They helped to look after the animals and worked in the fields or garden. Boys chopped wood and brought in water. Girls milked cows, weeded fields, and collected eggs from their family's hens. They also worked in the house by sewing, cooking, and doing laundry.

Pioneer girls helped their mothers do all the household chores.

DID YOU KNOW?
Pioneer women used a spinning wheel to make yarn for weaving and knitting.

23

First Nations and the pioneers

First Nations people were already living on the land when the pioneers arrived. Some First Nations people helped the pioneers. They showed pioneers how to find food such as berries and to hunt in the woods.

First Nations people showed the pioneers how to make useful items such as moccasins and canoes.

DID YOU KNOW?

The First Nations people called beans, corn, and squash "The Three Sisters." A legend says these foods will grow well only if they are planted together.

The **First Nations** people taught the pioneers how to make medicine from plants. They also taught the pioneers how to make maple syrup and maple sugar. Maple treats made food taste better.

The pioneers collected sap from the maple trees. Pioneers boiled the sap to make maple syrup and maple sugar.

DID YOU KNOW?

The First Nations people taught the pioneers useful ways to travel in the **wilderness**. This included using snowshoes, moccasins, birch bark canoes, and toboggans.

Making butter

Pioneer families who had cows could make their own butter. You can make butter too.

What you need:

- a 250 mL carton of 35% whipping cream
- a glass jar with a screw-on lid (like an old jam jar)
- a colander
- a bowl
- a wooden spoon
- a pinch of salt

What to do:

1. Pour the whipping cream into the jar. It should be one half to three fourths full.

2. Screw on the lid.

3. Start shaking the jar. After about 10 minutes, you will see the cream get foamy. Keep shaking.

4. Soon a thin liquid will appear. This is buttermilk. Shake until the bits of butter stick together and make a lump.

5. Put the colander over the bowl and pour in the buttermilk and butter.

6. Put the butter into a bowl and use the wooden spoon to mix in a little bit of salt. Enjoy your butter!

Glossary

apron cloth draped over a person's clothes and tied at the back. An apron protects the wearer from dirt or spilled food.

bonnet hat that is tied under the chin with ribbons and covers the whole head, but not the face

chores work done on the farm or around the house

crops plants that are grown and harvested for food

First Nations people who have lived in Canada for thousands of years

flax plant that is grown to make linen cloth or to feed animals

forage to search for food in the wild

harvest gathering crops after they are grown

mill building with machinery to grind, crush, or cut material

wilderness original land that has not yet been settled; it may be used by First Nations people

Find out more

Books

Pioneer Kids, Frieda Wishinksy (OwlKids, 2007)

The Kids Book of Canadian Exploration, Anne-Maureen Owens and Jabe Yealland (Kids Can Press, 2008)

Websites

FactHound offers a safe, fun way to find Internet sites related to this book. All of the sites on FactHound have been researched by our staff.

Here's all you do:

Visit www.facthound.com
Type in this code: 9781410981189

Index